1618

THE
OVERTURE
REPRIEVE

ALEXANDER ANGLISS

Cover image: - *Caspar David Friedrich, Wanderer Above the Sea of Fog (1818)*

The Overture Reprieve

Independently published by Alexander Angliss

Southampton 2022

ISBN: 9798846815100

DEDICATIONS

My fiancée
My friends
My family

"To Love and Happiness Forever"

CONTENTS

FIRST- FORGOTTEN LIGHT.

LET ME KNOW WHEN.

Let me know when to rule and when to reign

Or trust, when to echo and when to fade,

When may one rise and know the hour to wane

Towards perditions once, by self, forbade.

How's a man to hide away his virtue

And what's a man too shy about his grace?

What lies within he may dare to nurture?

How far can he those faded steps, retrace?

If strength's the will by which he holds on,

How's he then to train sinews to let go?

And still rebuild what others have seen gone

Showing not the nerves they begged him grow?

Let me know what I'd do, that you would not

Tell me what I must keep, and what to let rot.

ONWARD.

Faltered and blundered,

half-paced, he moves me

calling, "Onward…Onward"

in nightmare and dreams,

It's true my father seems

but to be

periphery.

And yet he calls me

Onward.

Fury crying,

I see too well that Father dying,

"Onward, Onward,

we are not yet truly sundered."

Rage…Rage,

and whisper.

Once, He told me,

how he missed her.

I told him backwards,

Onward.

Fury.

Crying.

You are dead and I am dying.

And Ghost speech is calling,

"Onward."

Father- Dream,

drift and rest in me.

Commit yourself,

to memory,

To echo, never saying

"Onward, Onward,

my son, bloody

nothing worth."

No more, forsake my birth.

And bid, I antically dispose,

why did your dreams transpose?

I cannot for my woes

suggest with heavenly shows,

it's good to travel onward.

Nor retain that spark,

to which my wonders bark,

Polymetis,

Alexander.

Mark.

THINGS I CAN'T TALK ABOUT

BECAUSE I ACCIDENTALLY LAUGH
SOMETIMES,

BECAUSE THEY SEEM LIKE LIES

AND IT'S REALLY RATHER EMBARRASING-

THE POEM.

This is today's memory:

My mother once tried to eat

my father's brains,

off of my hand.

But it may have simply been

coagulated blood.

It seems

that all who never had it

on their hand

say that.

THAT'S WHAT FRIENDS ARE FOR.

I detest your dreams of station,

beneath a few others.

Strong guys,

with whom you are safe.

As you've then forever,

a thousand fathers to come to call

the curtain,

so, you'll need never

own the stage.

And need not look at me,

applauding.

You dare not see a brother,

sure enough to do it all.

Because you are on a leash,

which shall reach just shy,

of the object of your eye.

Never given cause

to ask,

to reason

why

You long but be a little

greater

than I.

REAL TRAIN.

I'm sort of a passenger

On a real train,

Dreaming

Of stops between

My stations.

Choo Choo.

*SECOND- FOR OTHERS,
BURNS TOO BRIGHT.*

THIS IS HOW YOU PRAY.

All the daws of amour

peck at us.

All the wolves are howling

charnel songs of lust.

I hear the bells of heaven tolling

for some twisted cause.

They trust

to render

prostrate,

silence,

dust.

Treasonous,

to speak the name of thee

Divinity.

THE LAST NIGHT UNDER THE MORNING STAR.

The last night   Under the morning star
She caved caress   With her serpent too
In shadow   Routed in her fruits
She inward drew   In oppositions
The sword   Of heaven

Of life
Of breath
Of love
Of death

AT WAR WITH THE THEATRE OF LOVE.

Beyond longing,

I've seen you burn,

in fire tempest

null for me.

A world

of passions,

reasons- madness

coy and dancing,

strange delights,

Where you, old love,

are sweet

on curtains

come to call on lost

and amorous traditions.

Yet they've forever stayed

on open.

Though music scarcely plays

you off the stage.

My girl you are

a beautiful thing.

For all you are

and all I'd love

to never be

again.

HURRAY TO KNOWLEDGE.

Hurray to knowledge.

Sister soul I love you,

ever tracing

tantric dances

born of words'

sweet dreams.

Though now

unscrawled, the secret seems

but to be

some meek delight.

And by the by,

another night

has stepped aside

for me to come,

to seek,

to sing,

to touch,

loves lines

on your memory.

so, I am dancing now

where we hung,

the kiss,

its sleep,

the dream,

The Overture Reprieve.

A MOONBEAM FROM LIGHTNING.

I'll soon confess,

I talk too much

in riddles.

Though I'd sooner have you know,

I love by none.

I think, perchance,

my loves are proven

worn and sleeved enough

to tell it all-

I do not love in jest.

Whilst at times

I'm false in fashions,

serving but to call on muses, yes.

I'm not belied

within my passions.

A heart too often won

is scarcely kept

and for you, my girl,

I know, I've never writ

and never wept.

THIRD- A FLAME ALONE IN DARK.

NECTAR.

Had you a thorn, I'd long not for a rose,

Or held some mad nectar, I'd need not drink

And were you not so blind, I'd need not pose.

Had you less heart I'd long, far less, to think,

And had you looked on diamonds with my eyes,

Had you listened, heard music merely play,

I'd need not show you much, nor talk too wise

Or lay with you nightly to mock the day.

I would just love for you to never dance

In that lineated space of flowers,

Where the voices listened to have no chance,

to sing, to speak, to bring forth their powers.

For you'd have lent your worth another measure.

Let drift those things that we have come to treasure.

MNEMOSONYE

Mother muse,

come unto me.

And be thine

-mine,

restlessly, eternal.

Laid bare

and here.

Betwixt and in me

everlasting.

Hazy growing,

prophetic, casting

light in speech.

Grant me stars

and sacred daughters

and be between,

my glass

and sheets,

in dancing

happy hours.

Ancient lover,

Mnemosyne,

come unto me.

Once more to fate,

love mother,

Memory.

TERPSICHORE.

Circle sweetly.

Race fate.

Mock stillness.

Create,

liminal space.

Dance

and dream

for me

Terpsichore.

Rage and laugh

and grace

each shape

We take,

With the politic

of heavenly body.

And bare each kiss

to teach

morphology,

within the dream

Of me.

BORROWED TONGUES.

My love, talk slow. Whisper to me gently.

Soft words shall withstand passions' fevered heat.

Dreams of song and screaming speech have spent me.

Disquiet emotion too long composed the suite.

I've only curses spun upon a blackened tongue.

I stole from muses, songs that only gods have sung.

All my reason ran, too fast, with madness

so, my words became too much alike my pace.

Wishing only for loves dance with sadness.

Racing too fast to spy its secret space.

Unbend my ear once more and let me hear you.

In the simplest forms, you've coyly taken.

Forget the dreams that we have moved through.

Whisper truth and prove I was mistaken.

SILENCE.

Silence the muse.

Release her.

Let nothing beat.

Blacken the tongue.

Congeal the heart.

Sew pitch within the seed.

She downs the dark

and drowns the night

and clips the wings of dream.

Yet only the vaguest

of speech shall part

Those lips.

So, I dare not speak

so long

as voice is but a loan from love.

I give my piece.

- A word.
- A name
- A dream
- A word
- A name-
  rose sweet.

Though they never such lips

meet.

Silence the muse.

Let nothing beat.

FOURTH- THE BRIGHTEST, BLUE IN HEART.

BAD VIBRATIONS.

Lay with vision

and me.

Line loves diamonds

like some dream,

shining.

Play beneath,

that vision of me,

Hard- charged,

alike all electric

things. Come,

to count your sheep.

Once more to dream.

Once more to dream.

Thereafter mine

and memory.

One word uttered,

brief,

and lightly spoken.

I see you,

speak of me.

Always saying

 Something strange,

just there,

beneath,

in the sinewous pines,

 of midnight's reach.

Wherein

I am vison,

and I

am dream.

and I am

probably

Still

quite sweet,

about you.

Tenderly unstuck…

In the dream of her,

I drift delight,

and trace to pass.

Sunbeam dreams and memories,

are like

my shadow and her shape.

set to kiss

again, and again.

We gain,

all our yesterdays.

We touch:

- Slow trains,
- Homeward Journeys,
- Crawling,
- Lust.

Longing for the words,

perchance,

to grasp,

the smoke of amorous thought,

the mirrors seen through happy hours,

unto dusk.

So, after

stars can tell of sparce

and secret things,

well known to court the light.

Tenderly unstuck,

in the dream of her,

I drift delight.

CHEERS?

Only I'm still drinking.

Speaking just

to take

a chance.

Everybody's begging

me to raise

my glass.

Or be quiet a minute.

Raise my sword,

and swing,

saying something,

I really mean - I really believe?

I can?

When

if then,

we kiss, we dance?

There's truth

 in me perhaps.

Something like that?

Somewhere herein, lies

and inspiration.

Trance?

I love

and I love

and I am still

just a man.

THE MIDNIGHT LOVERS GLADE

PART ONE.

Between the creases of enveloping night,

withdraw to me.

Betwixt the sheets of endless dark,

provide me some Vision.

Silhouette,

passion's flame in secret midnight,

where you dare sing

sweetly witching,

words and trance thereafter memory.

Around, before, beside,

even beyond,

the stars do the nocturns sameness,

Reiterate,

identically unchanged.

within the sacred folds of everlasting,

omniscient dreams,

do our will and make

blindness,

the brightest guide, to seek in darkness:

The Midnight Lovers Glade.

THE MIDNIGHT LOVERS GLADE
PART TWO.

Withdraw to me,

to the twilight of eternal dawn,

to the dayless place,

where your flowers shall know

only sun.

Where stars waning die,

and are born,

to a sky of black.

and in deathbirth ever forgetting,

just how your roses grow.

Rather,

longing

instead,

just for your thorns.

So, withdraw from sleep.

Remember the dusk

and amber dreams.

There's few who dare

to never know

Asphodel's touch.

But there's another green

which welled out

from my forlorn skies

and rested in your raven eyes.

With tears, go down,

and down,

and down unto those promised stars.

Towards that secret

midnight place,

where the tungsten moon's the bones

Of fallen lover's

Silver Sun.

Return to dusk

and dawn.

Withdraw once more.

Retreat

beneath the trees,

outside the Starlight Hearth,

where we are

never chaste.

Where Daphne's spirit

daughters bathe

and sing.

Whilst fates are weaved,

by rights of Muse's lust

and sinewous words,

which speak of love,

and dream

and sinful night.

FIFTH- THE STRONGEST, SHINING SHIELD.

SALT TEARS.

I beseech
some part
of your heavens now.

For the first time
I'm possessed,
by Love
bearing out,
from no lamentable strain.

Held close by some amorous will,
borne not within me
but through me.

And unfolding into you,
like aether,
I move
into more than dreams
of you.

Whilst ghosts
and shadows
and reflections,
cast into the salt tears
of the earth
and the dust,
which waits
and claims us
its children.

And into the clay,
from which we are made
and the fire secret which made us,
alike the intimations
of mystery
and the workings of her dusk.

Yet it seems certain,
I need not those arrivals
to complete myself.

For you are seeming now
the very breath of life
and you are living me.

PROMETHEUS ABOUNDS?

There's not much sense

in asking water

to hold water.

Fire

to catch fire.

Nor high winds

to cradle a breeze.

They're already doing so.

I'm know, I'm sure to beg you,

coalesce,

hold me close,

guide me home.

And yet rains know not,

what tempest wrought them

or what storms await.

If storms await.

I suppose in truth,

there's naught in me,

that holds

the right, to bid you

catch

my smoke.

Or put out fires.

You have come

from fires too.

It matters not

if at times

we are each too different

or but

too much the same.

Sometimes I am fire

and sometimes you are rain.

EPILOGUE.

FIRST-
 FORGOTTEN LIGHT

SECOND-
 FOR OTHERS BURNS TOO BRIGHT

THIRD-
 A FLAME ALONE IN DARK

FOURTH-
 THE BRIGHTEST, BLUE IN HEART

FIFTH-
 THE STRONG AND SHINING SHIELD

BEFORE THE FIVE SHALL DARKNESS YIELD!

<u>*AFTERWORD*</u>

This text (not accounting for the whims, necessities, and imaginations of poetic license) is a rather personal text. It presents a speaker who comes from a place of loneliness, trauma, and anger. A place which he repeatedly attempts to leave however, in doing so he becomes harmful selfish and nihilistic. This damages the few precious relationships he has. Love becomes self-deprecation and self-deprecation becomes arrogance and vanity. It is not until he finally begins to recognize the merits of the people around him, that he manages an earnest attempt at change. Despite this attempt, he is continually failing these people and spiraling into old patterns of thought and desire. He becomes increasingly hurtful to his loved ones. Eventually however, he manages to follow the advice of the people he loves enough to discover his place of personal power and reflection. It is his dream and his glade of midnight and yet, he only allows the people he loves within upon invitation. This proves inadequate as it is these people which wrought its construction. This glade, this liminal space, at which he arrives is, at times, to me a metaphor   for the precious personal fortitude I have erected within myself as a consequence of the love and compassion of those people to whom I have dedicated this book.

They have served me the impetus to be a better man.

I suppose in some ways, this is that story. It may be

often   unfinished,   constantly   unglamorous,   and
uncharming; however, if I have learned one thing in
the production of this text, it is that a man's better
halves   mean   nothing   if   isolated   from   the   muses
which have wrought them. I give this book with love
and gratitude to these people. It is my invitation, for
all   time,   always.

ABOUT THE AUTHOR

Alexander Angliss was born in Hampshire, England in 1999. He is currently studying English Literature at the University of Winchester. The Overture Reprieve is his literary debut. He has a particular passion for poetry and hopes that this text is the first of many.

The Business Context

London: The Stationery Office

Published with the permission of the Central Computer and Telecommunications Agency on behalf of the Controller of Her Majesty's Stationery Office.

© Crown Copyright 2000

First published 2000

ISBN 0 11 330872 8

Titles within the Business Systems Development series include:

SSADM Foundation	ISBN 0 11 330870 1
Data Modelling	ISBN 0 11 330871 X
The Business Context	ISBN 0 11 330872 8
User-Centred Design	ISBN 0 11 330873 6
Behaviour and Process Modelling	ISBN 0 11 330874 4
Function Modelling	ISBN 0 11 330875 2
Database and Physical Process Design	ISBN 0 11 330876 0
Also available as a boxed set	ISBN 0 11 330883 3

For further information on CCTA products
Contact:

CCTA Help Desk
Rosebery Court
St Andrews Business Park
Norwich NR7 0HS
Tel 01603 704567 GTN 3040 4567

CONTENTS

FOREWORD

The Business Systems Development (BSD) series represents 'best practice' approaches to investigating, modelling and specifying Information Systems. The techniques described within this series have been used on systems development projects for a number of years, and a substantial amount of experience has contributed to the development of this guidance.

Within the BSD series the techniques are organised into groups that cover specific areas of the development process, for example *User Centred Design* which covers all aspects of the investigation, specification and design of the user interface.

The techniques provide a practical approach to the analysis and design of IT systems. They can also be used in conjunction with other complementary techniques such as Object-Oriented techniques.

The material used within this series originated in the Structured Systems Analysis and Design Method (SSADM) which was introduced by the CCTA as a standard method for the development of medium to large IT systems. Since its introduction in the early 1980s, SSADM has been developed through a number of versions to keep pace with the evolving technology and approaches in the IT industry.

The SSADM Foundation volume within the BSD series describes the basic concepts of the method and the way in which it can be employed on projects. It also describes how the different techniques can be used in combination.

Each of the other volumes in the series describes techniques and approaches for developing elements of the overall specification and design. These can be used in conjunction with one another or as part of alternative approaches. Cross-referencing is provided in outline within the description of each of the techniques to give pointers to the other approaches and techniques that should be considered for use in combination with the one being described.

All volumes within the Business System Development series are available from:

The Stationery Office
St Crispins
Duke Street
Norwich
NR3 1PD

Acknowledgments

Laurence Slater of Slater Consulting Ltd is acknowledged for editing existing material and, where necessary, developing new material for the volumes within the Business System Development series. John Hall, Jennifer Stapleton, Caroline Slater and Ian Clowes are acknowledged for much of the original material on which this series is based.

The following are thanked for their contribution and co-operation in the development of this series:

Paul Turner	Parity Training
Tony Jenkins	Parity Training
Caroline Slater	Slater Consulting Ltd

In addition to those named above, a number of people agreed to review aspects of the series and are thanked accordingly.

1   INTRODUCTION

Requirements defined for a new automated system will be of a better quality if they are based on knowledge of what users are required to do within the business environment, and what information they need. Requirements definition will be better still if the analyst can understand why the users do what they do, and how different users business activities are related. This understanding should improve consistency and provide a sound basis for the rest of the project.

IT application projects are mainly focused on the automated information system to be developed. Explicit description of business activities is generally outside their scope; in the development of Data Flow Models, for example, one of the steps is to move manual activity outside the system boundary (where *system* here means *automated information system*).

It is extremely useful to have an explicit model of business activities, to ensure that requirements to be met by the information system are complete and consistent, and will provide support for coherent user jobs. If there is no explicit model, description of business activities will be spread across a number of analysis and design products with the result that validation of a basic understanding of the business is very difficult.

This volume is concerned with the modelling of the business within an IT project from which an understanding of requirements is derived. It covers two aspects, these being:

- Business Activity Modelling;

- Requirements Definition.

Business Activity Modelling documents the essential activities that need to be undertaken within the business together with the business events that trigger the activities and the business rules that indicate how an activity is undertaken. This will aid the analyst in understanding how a new system will fit into the overall picture of the business.

Requirements Definition is concerned with documenting requirements for any new IT system.

It should be noted that the concepts, products and techniques described in this volume are concerned with modelling business processes as part of an IT project and not for their own sake. There may be projects undertaken within the Organisation which are focused on modelling business processes in order to understand or re-design the way in which the business operates (e.g., a business process re-engineering project). If this is so, these other projects may provide a useful starting point for Business Activity Modelling and Requirements Definition.

In this series all products are shown in the context of the System Development Template (SDT). This is a template which divides the system development process into activity areas onto which the development products may be mapped. Annexe A provides a fuller description of the System Development Template. Business Activity Modelling and Requirements Definition are undertaken in the Investigation area of the System Development template as shown in Figure 1-1.

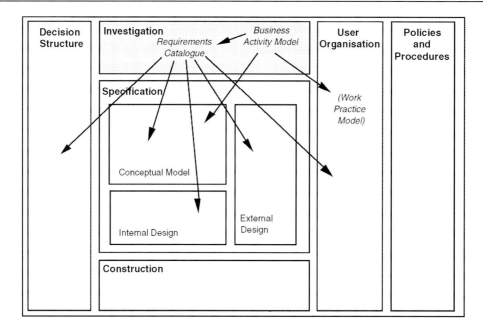

Figure 1-1 Place of Business Activity Modelling and Requirements Definition products in the System Development Template

The diagram shows that the Business Activity Model (the product of Business Activity Modelling) and the Requirements Catalogue (the product of Requirements Definition) have impacts in most other areas of the System Development Template. The Requirements Catalogue, in particular, is a product which is maintained throughout the project as a central reference point for what is required in the new system.

 All the examples within this volume are described in terms of EU-Rent which is a case study based around a car-rental business. For a full description of EU-Rent, see Annexe B.

The Business Activity Model and Information Support

The Business Activity Model represents a system[1] of business activities which will be supported by an information system. Its purpose is to act as the basis for deriving requirements for that information system. The information system covers all the stored information that is needed by business activities and can contain non-automated information sources as well as IT support.

An IT system can be used to support business activities in two ways:

- to perform business activities (or portions of business activities);
- to provide information to business activities.

---

[1] Note that the term *system* is used to describe the business activities being modelled. This is because it is expected that business activities are connected, co-ordinated and directed at some common purpose.

The Business Activity Model should be a central source of requirements for a new automated information system. Requirements for an IT project are derived by identifying the information support needed by the business activities, as represented in Figure 1-2.

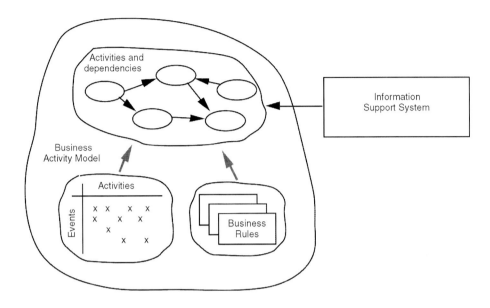

Figure 1-2 Information support for business activity

Where an automated system is being developed to support business activities, the information support to business activities will be sub-divided further when the boundary of the automated system is decided, as shown in Figure 1-3. This sub-division is done by consideration of the following:

- distinguishing between IT and non-IT information support;

- identifying additional activities (i.e., not part of the basic set of business activities) needed to acquire the information to keep the IS up to date (striped in Figure 1-3);

- automating business activities (shaded in Figure 1-3).

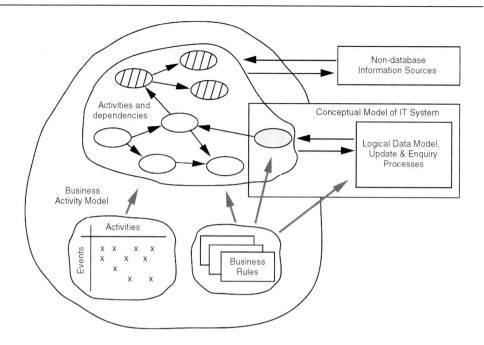

Figure 1-3 Different types of Information Support

To develop a specification of the requirements for a new automated system, it is necessary to separate categories of information which are to be provided by the new system from those which will be provided from elsewhere. The separation is unlikely to be clear-cut when the Business Activity Model is first developed and requirements are first defined. There will be a need to refine these as the project progresses.

For example, to give directions to customers, EU-Rent branches need maps and local street guides. EU-Rent could provide automated geographical information, or branches could buy copies of published maps and directories. For customer credit status, counter staff will have on-line access to credit card companies, which might be provided via the workstation for the IT system to be developed, or via a separate card-swipe terminal.

Some business activities can potentially be automated. Any activity which does not require a decision or direct intervention by a user will be a candidate for automation. For example, in the EU-Rent system, the allocation of specific cars to rentals could be automated, based on rules that can be automatically applied, such as allocating high-tariff groups before low-tariff groups and giving free upgrades to customers in the benefits system where no cars of the required car group are available. Alternatively, the user may simply require the system to provide a list of rentals and a list of available cars with the matching being performed by the booking clerks.

By examining the information that is required by business activities, it should be possible to identify the business activities that maintain this information. Many of the required inputs will be provided by activities that are directly associated with satisfying the overall purpose of the system. However, there may be a need to introduce further business activities to obtain the required information to keep the base of information up to date.

Business Activities in the Business System

The Business Activity Model is not a complete picture of the business under investigation. It concentrates solely on the essential activities independent of the organisation structure and 'who does what'. A description of the total business system (or Work Practice Model) would need to supplement the Business Activity Model by mapping it onto the user organisation. This is represented in Figure 1-4.

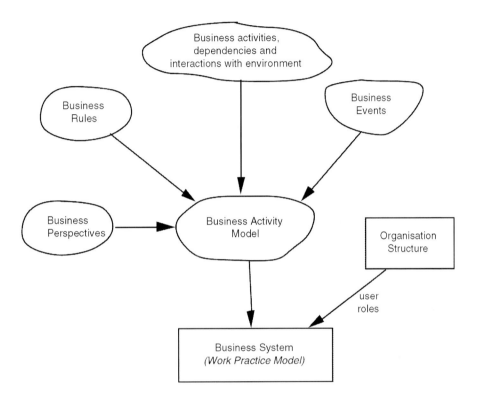

Figure 1-4 Mapping of Business Activity Model onto Organisation Structure

Organisation Structure

The Organisation Structure will define who will be performing the business activities, the 'actors' in the business system. For business activities which require automated support, the actors will be a combination of human and computer. The identification of the human actors involved in activities requiring automated support can assist in the identification of users and user roles for the new IT system.

Who does what

What is done should be clearly separate from who does it. It should be possible to change the organisational structure without changing the business activity.

The mapping of business activities onto the user organisation is part of the Work Practice Model which is described in the *User Centred Design* volume in this series.

Organisation of this volume

After this (introductory) chapter the organisation for this volume is as follows:

Chapter 2 – Business Activity Modelling. This a full description of the concepts, products and techniques necessary for Business Activity Modelling.

Chapter 3 – Requirements Definition. This is a full description of the concepts, products and techniques necessary for Requirements Definition.

Chapter 4 – Meta-model. To assist projects and CASE tool developers, a meta-model is provided which shows the basic concepts covered in this volume and the way in which they inter-relate.

Chapter 5 – Product Descriptions. Product descriptions are provided for all the major products described in this volume. These should be used by projects as a basis for their product descriptions. (Note: It is expected that the project will need to tailor these product descriptions omitting any items that are not required and including any extra ones that are specific to the project.)

Annexes. There are three annexes appended to this volume. The first gives a description of The System Development Template, the second is a description of EU-Rent which is the case study that is used throughout the volume. The third is a glossary of terms that are relevant to this volume.

2   BUSINESS ACTIVITY MODELLING

Information systems are built to support business activity. Business activities are generally not the same as information system activities. For example, in EU-Rent, the business activity 'buy cars' is supported by information system activities such as 'report on available stocks of cars and projected demand', 'respond to enquiries on models and prices', 'record purchasing decisions and expected delivery dates', 'print purchase orders' etc.

A Business Activity Model explicitly models what goes on in the business independently of how it will be supported by an information system. Its main purpose is to enable the analyst to identify and document requirements directly from the needs of business activities. This helps to ensure that:

- the degree of subjectivity is reduced such that the new computer system will meet the objectives of the business and not simply re-implement the current system or be constrained by specific perspectives of certain users;

- the design of the IT system will be user centred; the services that the IT system will provide will be designed to support whole user jobs, rather than the IT-system-centred view that a set of enquiries and updates has to be provided, to be used as needed by authorised users.

A Business Activity Model describes the activities which are essential for the business to be able to meet a particular objective, or set of objectives. These activities are independent of the Organisational Structure and the allocation of tasks to individuals. Assignments of activities to user roles and locations are made in the Work Practice Model (covered in the *User Centred Design* volume in this series).

The Business Activity Model is defined in Investigation in the System Development Template, as a major input to Requirements Definition. This is illustrated in Figure 2-1. It is directly related to the Conceptual Model in Specification, and indirectly, via the Work Practice Model, to the External Design.

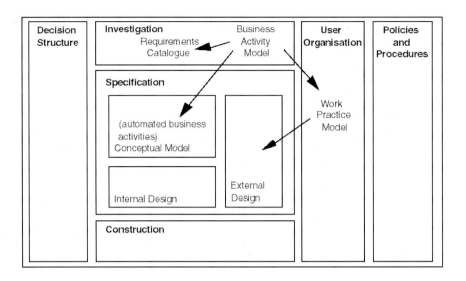

Figure 2-1 Business Activity Model in the System Development Template

There are several well-established approaches to modelling business activity that can be used to produce the Business Activity Model and each organisation should decide on the technique that will be most appropriate for its use. This chapter describes the concepts covered by a Business Activity Model and then gives examples from techniques that can be used for developing the Business Activity Model. It should be noted that other techniques for Business Activity Modelling are just as valid providing the basic concepts of the Business Activity Model are covered.

The Business Activity Model for a project is developed within a defined scope which is determined in a higher-level business planning and analysis exercise, or within business and IS strategies. There may be other Business Activity Models with which it has to be co-ordinated. They may be part of a wider business scope, or with different functional scope within the same business area. For example, EU-Rent car rentals has to be co-ordinated with:

- EU-Corporation's other businesses, EU-Stay (hotels) and EU-Fly (airline);

- parallel EU-Rent business activities such as acquiring and maintaining premises; recruiting, training and paying staff.

2.1   The Concepts of Business Activity Modelling

2.1.1 Business perspectives – why the business is doing what it does

When developing IT systems to support business activities, it can be assumed that everyone within the business shares a belief about the basic function of the business. For example, when developing IT systems to support the business of EU-Rent, it must be assumed that EU-Corporation believes that renting cars is a worthwhile business to be in. If EU-Corporation's belief was that it was in business to generate profits, regardless of what business activity generated those profits, an option would be to sell the car rental business and put the proceeds into another business area. In this case, EU-Corporation should be having a business review of car rentals, rather than a project to provide IT support for it.

A business perspective is a particular slant on this shared belief. The shared belief can be assumed, but there will be different views about the overall objectives required in order to make the business function in accord with the belief. For example, for EU-Rent, once the assumption is made that this is a car rental business, one perspective may be expressed as follows:

"… and car rental customers want value for money, rather than the lowest possible prices"

In almost all business systems there will be multiple perspectives, which may conflict. For example, in EU-Rent:

"... and car rental customers want low rates and no frills"

" ... but the competition doesn't give us much room for manoeuvre on price; we should concentrate on looking after cars well and selling them at the right time, to minimise depreciation"

The stated business perspectives will help to identify what factors will be important in ensuring the success of the business (critical success factors). For example, some factors that will be important in the EU-Rent system will include the following:

- knowing what customers perceive as 'value for money' and delivering it;
- keeping prices in line with the competition;
- minimising depreciation.

Some critical success factors will be specific to the business area being modelled, others may be inherited from higher-level analysis and planning activities. For example, 'value for money' is likely to be part of EU-Corporation's marketing presentation across all its service businesses.

2.1.2 Business Activities – what is done

Business activity does not exist in isolation. It is embedded in an environment - the outside world and, perhaps, other parts of the same business - with which it must interact. Business activity is activity directed to some explicit purpose, such as renting cars, collecting tax revenue, treating patients, providing social security benefits. This explicit purpose can be called the **primary task**.

The different types of business activities are illustrated in Figure 2-2.

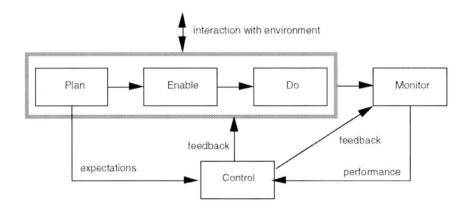

Figure 2-2 Concepts incorporated in a Business Activity Model

There must be *doing* activities – essential parts of the primary task. In EU-Rent, these would include allocating cars to customers, handing them over, reclaiming them at the end of the rental, and obtaining the rental fee.

There must also be enabling activities, which ensure that the resources and facilities needed by the doing activities are available. In EU-Rent, these would include purchasing cars, attracting customers, servicing cars, moving cars to where they are needed.

As is illustrated in Figure 2-2 the *doing* and *enabling* activities must be planned thus introducing the concept of the *planning* activities. In EU-Rent, planning activities would include deciding what car models to offer, how many cars of each to buy, how many cars branches should own. Activities to define rules will be part of the planning activities. Some examples of rules are given in 'How activities are done', below . Planning activities also include setting performance expectations. In EU-Rent these would include expectations for car utilisation, for closeness of fit between demand and availability of car models, and for branch turnover and profit.

Planning, enabling and doing activities are monitored, and performance data is collected for comparison with expectations.

Planning, enabling, doing and monitoring activities are all controlled. Control activities act on other activities when performance expectations are not met. Consequently, they may require changes in what is monitored. For example, in EU-Rent, if branches were not meeting performance targets, control action might change numbers and mix of cars at branches, marketing positioning of EU-Rent's service, number of staff at branches and rules for allocating cars.

In many projects a major part of the requirements are concerned with improving IT support for planning and control action, and building in cost-effective monitoring.

The collection of all these activities is known as the **Logical Activity Model**.

2.1.3 Business Events - when activity is done

Business activities are triggered by business events.

Business events are of three types:

- external inputs – inputs from outside the system boundary

  In EU-Rent, externally input events include: advance request for a rental, delivery of car from manufacturer, walk-in rental, return of car from rental.

- decisions made in business activities within the system

  In EU-Rent, internal decisions include: change of rates in rental tariff, write-off or repair of damaged car, suspension of customer.

- scheduled points in time

  In EU-Rent, scheduled points include: start of working day (customers are contacted for any cars which were due, but not returned, the previous day), and end of working day (specific cars are allocated to rental bookings due for pick-up the next day).

A business event may trigger more than one activity. For example, in EU-Rent, the business event 'return of car from rental' triggers activities 'reclaim car', 'assign car for repair' (if it has been damaged while on rental), and 'collect rent'.

An activity may be triggered by more than one business event. For example, activity 'assess customer credit-worthiness' can be triggered by events 'rental request' (if the customer provides credit card details), 'rental pick-up' and 'walk-in rental'.

Also, it is often possible to identify a set of business events and business activities which represent a 'business thread'. A business thread can be recognised as the path through a set of business activities which are the outcome of an initiating business event. A thread does not need to be continuous in its progression, but may need further business events to trigger later business activities. For example, in the EU-Rent system, an initial business event Rental Request triggers some business activities immediately but also leads to a series of business activities triggered by further business events:

- end of day before pick-up: triggers allocation of car to reservation;

- pick-up: triggers credit and driving licence checking and release of car;
- rental return: triggers recovery of car, charging for rental, and, if car has been damaged during rental, scheduling of car for repair.

All of these may be collected together into one business thread.

Note that there is not necessarily a one-to-one correspondence between business events and the IS events. For example, the business events 'customer death', 'customer bankruptcy', 'EU-Rent management decision not to do any more business with customer' might all be represented by the IS event 'customer termination' (perhaps accompanied by text giving a reason for the termination). The business event 'get minor repair done by local garage and pay for it out of petty cash' might not appear as an IS event at all.

2.1.4 Business Rules – how activities are done

For many activities there are explicit rules for how activities are done.

Rules are of two types - constraints and operational guidance.

Constraints

Constraints define conditions under which an activity cannot be done or conditions under which an activity must be done.

Constraints may be imposed externally, from the outside world or from other parts of the business, or set within the Business Activity Model. Those that are defined within the Business Activity Model may potentially be changed by control actions.

In EU-Rent, outside world constraints include: 'drivers must have a valid driving licence', 'rented cars must be road-worthy'. Constraints set by policy in other parts of the business include 'only car models on the approved list may be ordered by branches', 'cars must be picked up and dropped off in the same country', 'each customer in the benefit scheme must be sent a statement at least once per year'.

Business defined constraints include: 'drivers must be over 25 and have held a full driving licence for at least a year', 'cars allocated to rentals must be physically present at the branch'.

Operational Guidance

Operational guidance determines how activities are done. It does not have to be defined procedurally.

Operational guidance may be defined externally, or within the Business Activity Model. Guidance provided from within the Business Activity Model may be changed by control actions.

In EU-Rent, external operational guidance includes what rate of VAT to charge, what to include on an invoice etc.

Internal operational guidance includes what to do when a car of the requested group is not available and how to decide when to sell cars.

Wherever rules are available, they should be referenced from the business activities. Note that rules do not have to be copied into the documentation; if they are well-documented elsewhere, for example in strategy documents, references should be adequate.

2.2   The Products of Business Activity Modelling

The Business Activity Model is the product of Business Activity Modelling. There is not one form for the model but it should include the following four areas:

1.   **Business Perspectives** – which is a statement of belief of what the business is trying to achieve.

2.   **Logical Activity Model** – which defines the activities to be carried out within the business in support of the primary task, their dependencies and the way in which they interact with the business environment.

3.   **Set of Business Events** – which are the triggers for the business activities.

4.   **Set of Business Rules** – which are the constraints and operational guidance under which the business activities work.

This is represented in Figure 2-3 below and described in the following chapters.

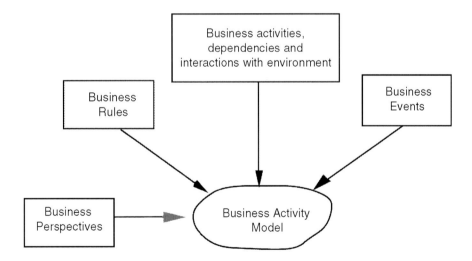

Figure 2-3 Schematic of Business Activity Model

2.2.1 Business Perspectives

There should be a statement of belief of what the business is achieving or could achieve. These are known as Business Perspectives.

Critical success factors, measures of performance and control action required to keep the business on track will all be based on business perspectives.

In most systems there are multiple business perspectives that have to be accommodated, which may require conflict-resolution activities (see below).

Note that business perspectives will normally be expressed in terms of the primary task of the business. In EU-Rent, they would be about car rental, or supporting activities such as car maintenance. Statements such as 'obtain acceptable return on investment', 'increase capital base by 10% per year' are measures of EU-Rent's performance in running a car rental business to meet management's and shareholders' expectations.

If 'to obtain acceptable return on investment' were the business perspective, then staying in the car rental business should not be a constraint. But a Business System Option that recommends "Sell all the cars and put the money into some more-profitable business" is not what EU-Rent's management expect from the project team.

2.2.2 The Logical Activity Model

The Logical Activity Model defines what activities have to be carried out, and the dependencies between them. Five types of activities are identified:

1. Doing Activities
2. Enabling Activities
3. Planning Activities
4. Monitoring Activities
5. Controlling Activities

These should fit the general structure illustrated in Figure 2-2.

Most approaches for modelling business activity will capture 'doing' and 'enabling' activities:

- **doing activities** contribute directly to the business purpose;

- **enabling activities** ensure that the resources and facilities needed by the 'doing' activities are available.

The selected approach must also capture the other elements in Figure 2-2, and have a means of documenting them:

- **planning activities** which plan how the enabling activities and doing activities will be carried out and define business expectations;

- **monitoring activities** which collect performance data for comparison with expectations;

- **control activities** which act on other activities when performance expectations are not met and, by doing this, may require changes in what is monitored.

In most systems there are multiple business perspectives that have to be accommodated and some of them may be in conflict. This would lead to a requirement for activities that resolve conflicts, e.g., 'decide when to discount and when to ask for the full rate', 'decide to postpone scheduled maintenance to meet a rental request', which will have to be supported by rules for users to follow or by users with authority to use their judgement. It is important to make conflict-resolution activities explicit; they can be crucial to the smooth running and success of the business, and may have special requirements for information support for decisions or definition of rules.

2.2.3 Set of Business Events

A business event is a trigger of one or more business activities. Business events are of three types:

- **external inputs** – often resulting from actions by people/groups outside the system boundary;

- **decisions made in business activities within the system** such as management and head-office actions;

- **scheduled points in time**, such as start of working day, end of financial year.

Unlike the IS concept of event, a business event does not necessarily affect stored data – it is simply a stimulus which causes business activities to be initiated.

For example, in EU-Rent, the business event Walk-in Rental Request triggers the business activities which check the customers driving licence and credit worthiness, allocate a car, get the customer to sign a credit card voucher and release the car to the customer.

Different business events can trigger the same business activities in different combinations and different sequences.

2.2.4 Set of Business Rules

Business rules should be explicitly documented within the Business Activity Model. The business activities state what is done whereas business rules define or support how business activities are done. Business rules are of two types:

- constraints

- operational guidance

Business activity should be supported by descriptions of constraints and operational guidance (where they are defined), or references to where they are documented. In some cases they will be references to general policies.

It is useful if the approach selected for modelling business activity documents business rules separately from the Logical Activity Model, but cross-referenced to activities within it. This would support re-use of rules in different activities (which may provide greater consistency in application of rules), and would allow different rules to be 'plugged in' to a Logical Activity Model as result of, say, control activity.

Some rules may be automated in the IT system; some will not, but may have to be provided (as text) in on-line help.

2.3   Approaches to Business Activity Modelling

Although the product of Business Activity Modelling – the Business Activity Model – is important in any project, the exact method of developing it is outside the scope of this publication. There are several well-established approaches for modelling business activity. One of them should be selected and used.

In this chapter, three different approaches are described as examples of Business Activity Modelling:

- Soft Systems Methodology;

- Business Analysis;

- Derivation of Business Activity Model from Resource Flow Diagrams.

It should be stressed that the above are not the only way to model business activities within a project. There are other business modelling methods that might be used, and this chapter should not be seen as an endorsement of any particular approach. Ideas from these approaches can be useful whether the full methods/approaches are used or not.

2.3.1 Using Soft Systems Methodology[2] for Business Activity Modelling

The Soft Systems Methodology (SSM) is directed at modelling of Human Activity Systems[3].

SSM can provide two of the components of the Business Activity Model:

- the business perspectives;

- the Logical Activity Model.

---

[2] see Systems: Concepts, Methodologies and Applications (second edition), Brian Wilson, Wiley, 1992.

[3] A Human Activity System is a coherent set of activities and the logical dependencies between them; it describes what has to be done in a business, as distinct from who does it and how it is done. It can be mapped on to an organisation structure to define a business system. In the mapping to an organisation, some of the activities in the human activity system may be automated. A Human Activity System needs information support, which is specified separately from the Human Activity System. Usually, only part of the information support will be provided by an IT system.

Business events and business rules can be captured using SSM products as a framework for investigation and specification, but they are outside the scope of SSM.

Overview of SSM

A 'hard' system requirement is a situation in which what is needed is known and the system specification has to address how to meet the requirement. A 'soft' system requirement is a situation in which what is needed has to be defined before addressing how it can be provided.

SSM addresses soft systems requirements. It is directed at business activity, and specifies IS requirements in terms of information support for business activity.

SSM's starting point is that what enterprises do can be described as 'human activity' systems - people working together in some coordinated way with a common purpose - but SSM does not attempt to model real-world activities directly. Instead, it uses a four-step approach:

1. create root definitions: statements of what the system is believed to be, by at least part of the population consulted (the business perspectives are captured here);

2. from each root definition derive a Primary Task Model of essential activities;

3. derive a consensus model that accommodates all relevant perspectives (the Logical Activity Model);

4. test the consensus model against reality.

Root Definition

Examples of Root Definitions from the EU-Rent System are:

*   "a system to produce acceptable return on investment by renting cars to the general public" (business perspective: it is possible to obtain acceptable financial return from a car rental business);

*   "a system to maintain loyalty of existing car rental customers by providing a high-quality service" (business perspective: high quality service ensures customer loyalty);

*   "a system to increase loyalty of existing car rental customers and attract new customers by providing a customer incentive scheme that compares well with those offered by EU-Rent's competitors" (business perspective: a competitive incentive scheme increases customer loyalty and attracts new customers).

A Root Definition does not have to express intent of the owners or operators of the Human Activity System. We might develop a Root Definition, defensible in observable reality, that is based on an undesirable business perspective. For example, in EU-Rent, "a system to wear cars out quickly by renting them for short periods to people who have no interest in taking care of them beyond the period of rental". The system owners would probably require that the effects of this Human Activity System be minimised!

Primary Task Model

The primary task is the common purpose to which the business activities are directed. The Primary Task Model of a Human Activity System defines what the system has to do in order to be the one defined in the Root Definition. The Primary Task Model is a coherent set of connected activities.

A Primary Task Model is derived formally from its Root Definition, and only from its Root Definition. It should not include any real-world activities that are not represented in the Root Definition.

An example of a high-level SSM Primary Task Model is given in Figure 2-4.

In the Primary Task Model, an arrow connecting two activities is a logical dependency. It means "in order for the activity at the head of the arrow to be going on, the activity at the tail of the arrow must also be going on". The arrow does not imply a trigger or an information flow (although, in some instances, that is what occurs in reality).

The 'Z' flows which do not point at other activities represent temporary dependencies on control activities - a control activity can affect any or all other activities within its scope (indicated by the shaded lines on Figure 2-4) in order that performance objectives are met.

"A system to provide a high-quality car rental service to the general public and operate a customer loyalty scheme, within legal constraints and company policies, while obtaining an acceptable return on investment "

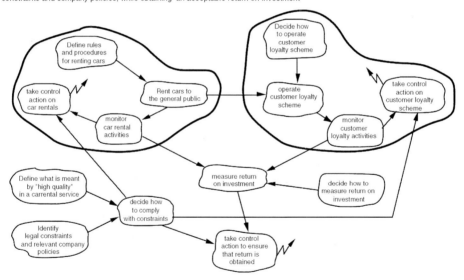

Figure 2-4 Example High-level Primary Task Model

The Consensus Model

An individual's viewpoint will consist of a mix of business perspectives with different weightings. For example, most EU-Rent branch managers will lean towards a perspective of always having to meet rental demand, but will recognise other perspectives; e.g. that the amount of capital tied up in cars must be minimised. Even when there are large numbers of individuals involved, all of their viewpoints can usually be captured in a relatively small number of Root Definitions.

SSM includes a procedure for combining the Primary Task Models for each of the Root Definitions to arrive at a consensus model. The important considerations are:

- there will be a 'neutral' set of activities common to all the models, since all are centred on the same business. In EU-Rent, all models have as their central activities the renting of cars to the general public;

- activities that appear on some models, but not on all, will have varying degrees of support from participating individuals. The analyst's job is to arrive at as wide-ranging an accommodation as possible;

- there may be conflicts between different perspectives, that have to be resolved (see below).

The resulting Consensus Primary Task Model is the Logical Activity Model.

Conflicting business perspectives

Sometimes business perspectives conflict with each other. For example, in the EU-Rent system, there is an apparent conflict between the requirement to maximise rental income and the wish to provide free rentals as part of the customer loyalty scheme.

When merging the primary task models into a single consensus model, there may be a need to introduce specific activities to resolve the conflicts between different perspectives.

Decomposition

Primary Task Models are hierarchical, each level showing more detail than the one above. Decomposition is based on the requirements for performance monitoring and control action. For decomposition, each model can be divided into a number of subsystems. Each subsystem is a subset of the activities for which, as a group, measures of performance, monitoring and control action can be defined.

Interactions with external systems and subsystems

A Human Activity System is not self-contained:

- first, it is a subsystem of a wider system, and interacts with other subsystems of the wider system. The EU-Rent system is a subsystem of:

    - the European car rentals market;

- ■ EU-Corporation's customer service business, which also includes EU-Stay (hotels) and EU-Fly (airline).

- second, there may be several co-existing and co-operating Human Activity Systems in a business enterprise. For example, from the EU-Rent Case Study, as well as the car rentals Human Activity System of EU-Rent there may be:

  - ■ a system to maintain EU-Rent premises in a state adequate for the conduct of its car rental business;

  - ■ a system to maintain staff competent to run EU-Rent's car rental business.

Comparing the Primary Task Model with reality

The Primary Task Model is developed independently of what is actually done in the real world. It can then be tested against what is done in the real world in order to highlight any problems.

There are two possible reasons for mismatches between the Human Activity System model and reality:

- the business perspective is invalid and the Root Definition does not describe a realisable situation – the world is not what the system owners and operators believed it to be. For example, from the EU-Rent system, one of the Root Definitions is "a system to maintain loyalty of existing car rental customers by providing a high-quality service" (business perspective: high quality service ensures customer loyalty). The reality may be that high quality service has no significant effect on customer loyalty – that low prices and frequent advertising maintain customer loyalty;

- real world activities are not consistent with the Primary Task Model and are therefore inconsistent with the Root Definition. In a real business situation, activities considered to be essential may be omitted, unnecessary activities may be done, some activities may not be controlled or activities may work against each other. For example, in the EU-Rent system, the reality of the customer benefits scheme may be a system that provides free services and gifts to car rental customers without any indication of whether this has any benefits to EU-Rent.

Whatever the reasons for the discrepancies, it is valuable for the system owners and operators to know that there are differences between reality and what they believe their business to be.

2.3.2 Business Analysis

Within IS projects, it is assumed that Business Activity Modelling starts from a definition of the business area that requires automated support. Business analysis methods can be used at a much earlier point in the systems development lifecycle to help in the understanding of the business and to suggest ways in which the business can be re-organised for better efficiency and effectiveness. Where business analysis has been undertaken prior to the identification of an IS project, these results can be used as a basis for the Business Activity Model.

There are generally three main stages to business analysis:

1. understanding the business area; this leads to the identification of the business perspectives;

2. defining and documenting what occurs within the business area; this leads to the identification of the business activities;

3. identification of business events.

The outcome of the exercise is an application development portfolio, which schedules the detailed system development projects.

Understanding the business area

In order to understand the business area, business analysis would be expected to identify the key issues that any information system should address. This involves examining how the business area relates to external entities such as customers and suppliers as well as other areas within the business. Such an investigation will help in identifying the objectives which the business area is trying to achieve, as well as the information that is necessary to plan and control the activities of the business area in order to achieve those objectives.

Identification of business activities

Functional Decomposition is a technique that is used widely in business analysis methods to model business activities. The approach starts with a high-level view of an organisation, sub-divided into a number of broad areas. Each area is analysed and a number of sub-areas identified. Each sub-area is then analysed and progressively decomposed until a detailed picture of business activities is developed.

There are two basic approaches to Functional Decomposition:

*   base the approach on the organisation/management structure, usually starting with an organisation chart;

*   identify a set of business streams within the organisation, for example product development, marketing, purchasing, production, sales, accounting. These are then made specific to the situation being studied.

This type of hierarchical model is usually relatively easy to develop and use. For example, Figure 2-5 illustrates part of a Functional Decomposition of EU-Rent, based on the current organisational responsibilities, which are mainly determined by the geography of the business.

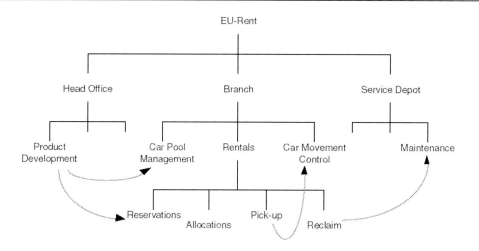

Figure 2-5 Functional decomposition

The hierarchy does not show the dependencies between activities in different substructures, some of which are shown by the broken arrows in the diagram. For example, Car Pool Management is dependent on the car models and the rental groups defined in Product Development. Reservations are dependent on the car groups and tariffs set in Product Development. Maintenance is dependent on Reclaim of cars – both mileage and damage are recorded when cars are returned. Car Movement Control is partly dependent on Pick-up; one-way rentals cause change of ownership of cars.

Identification of business events

Business events, and the resulting transactions are a familiar concept to users and the processes which handle them are set at the right kind of level for identifying systems. Whilst many business events, such as Customer Places Order, result in a clear transaction into a particular business area, other events such as Competitors Reduce Prices are not notified to us directly, but still have an impact and require a response.

The analyst should identify the business events to which the business area must respond. An event may indicate that there is a flow of information across the business area boundary, corresponding to the notification of the event and the area's reaction to the event. Any information flow into the area must be handled by a business activity, and any output flow must be produced by a business activity.

The results of the business event analysis could be compared with the lower-level processes defined from Functional Decomposition to ensure completeness. Furthermore, the analyst should always question the purpose of any activity. What would be the result of eliminating this particular activity? Is it really adding any value to the product or service that we are providing to our customers?

2.3.3 Using Resource Flow Diagrams

One approach for defining business activity is to start with the Resource Flow Diagram . The Resource Flow Diagram models the flow of physical resources around the current system and the processes which use those physical resources. Activities in the Resource Flow Diagram are business activities, not information system processes. A Resource Flow Diagram is particularly useful where the business uses very little IT (e.g., a paper based system) or where they have a large flow of physical resources (e.g., a car rental system).

An example of a Resource Flow Diagram from the EU-Rent system is given in Figure 2-6.

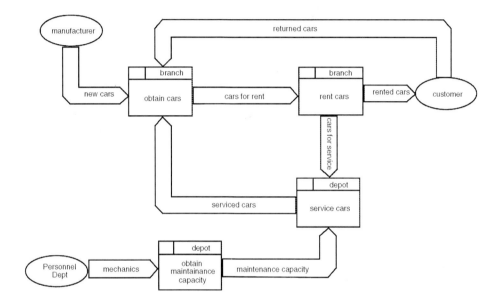

Figure 2-6 Example of Resource Flow Diagram

Comparing what is modelled in a Resource Flow Diagram with the Logical Activity Model shown in Figure 2-2, it can be seen that the coverage of Resource Flow Diagrams is incomplete:

- the Resource Flow Diagram is mainly concerned with doing (resources flowing outwards from the system) and enabling (resources flowing inwards to the system) activities;

- planning, monitoring and control activities are not usually shown; it is possible, however, to identify relevant information categories and the business activities that require them by asking a number of questions in relation to the Resource Flow Diagram.

Deriving Information Categories and Business Activities

Below is a checklist of questions that can be asked in relation to a Resource Flow Diagram. In response to each question, it should be possible to:

- name the business event (an information flow);

- state what has to be done (a business activity);

- specify whether the information flow should be provided by the required information system or comes from elsewhere.

It is usually easy to answer the 'doing' and 'enabling' questions. Answering the planning, monitoring and control questions may be more difficult, and answers in some areas may reflect what ought to be done rather than what is done now.

From the answers to the questions, it should then be possible to develop most of the components of a Business Activity Model:

- **Activities** should appear as operational (resource-handling) activities, or in response to questions. The dependencies between them have to be identified to create the Logical Activity Model. Guidance is provided in 'Building an activity model', below;

- **Business events** should mainly appear in responses to "what happens" questions in the checklist;

- Some **business rules** will appear in response to "what has to be done" questions. A second pass may be required, to ask, for each activity in the Logical Activity Model, what constraints and operational guidance exist.

- **Business perspectives** do not appear. The analyst has to develop them with the users and compare them with the Logical Activity Model.

Checklist of questions

'Doing' activities - providing resources

- What happens when a resource is requested?

- What happens when a resource is allocated in response to a request ?

- What happens when the allocated resource is delivered or handed over?

- Is the resource charged for within the scope of this system? If so:

  - What happens when payment is requested (and who is asked for it)?

  - What happens when payment is received?

'Enabling' activities - replenishing resources and identifying resource recipients

- What happens when the need to replenish a resource is identified?

- What happens when replenishment is requested?

- What happens when a replenishment of resource is received?

- What has to be done to transform incoming resource to resource to be provided?

- Is the resource paid for within the scope of this system? If so:

  - What happens when payment is requested (and who asks for it)?

  - What happens when payment is made?

- What has to be done to identify/authorise resource providers?

- What has to be done to identify/authorise resource recipients?

Planning activities

- What has to be done to decide what categories of resource should be offered?

- What has to be done to stay competitive?

- What has to be done to monitor use/consumption of resource?

- What has to be done to predict demand for resource?

- What has to be done to set performance expectations (of the business, not of the IT system)?

Monitoring activities

- What has to be done to monitor planning, enabling and doing activities?

- What has to be done to ensure that measures of performance can be collected?

Control activities

- What has to be done to identify constraints:

  - from outside the organisation (e.g. legal requirements)?

  - from inside the organisation (e.g. corporate policies)?

- What kinds of actions can be taken to modify business activities when performance expectations are not met, for example:

  - change business rules?

  - change resources?

  - change prices?

  - change expectations?

Building an activity model

Subsystem models for maintaining each type of resource

Subsystems should be identified, each of which is responsible for the provision and replenishment of a particular type of resource. Each subsystem should include activities for planning, enabling and doing what is required to obtain the required resources. In addition, activities should exist for monitoring and controlling these activities. Depending upon the type of system, other subsystems may be identified which deal with other aspects of the use of resources and their ultimate disposal.

Put subsystems together

The different subsystems identified above may need to be put together such that there is a logical dependency between them. In order to provide a resource, the resource must first be obtained and, perhaps, transformed.

Identify choices and conflicts

Are there any conflicts or choices in the model as developed so far, for example:

- if there are different kinds of resource that could be provided, there may be a choice of which to provide;

- demand may exceed supply. If so, is it necessary to make a choice of who to supply or is there an option of obtaining resource from elsewhere?

- there may be several different suppliers of resources. If so, who should we obtain resources from?

- an input resource may be used in a number of alternative transformations. If so, how much of the resource should be allocated to each transformation?

- there may be conflicting expectations within the system. If so, how is it possible to accommodate between them?

Where a choice is identified, there may be a need to add an activity which makes a decision or defines rules for making the choice. It is not necessary for the analyst to understand precisely how such activities work, but it is extremely useful to identify that such activities exist so that we can explore requirements for information support.

Define information support requirements for each activity

For each activity identified above, it should be possible to decide whether information is needed by that activity. If so, the source of that information should be determined from the following possibilities:

- directly from another business activity;

- from the outside world;

- from within the stored information system:

  - from data that is maintained by this system (what will be in the Logical Data Model);

  - from data which is kept within this system but is not maintained by the system. This category covers data that is 'bought-in' or acquired directly, such as telephone directories, CD-ROM, etc.;

  - via interfaces to other automated systems.

2.4 Relationship with other analysis and design techniques

2.4.1 Requirements Definition (covered in Chapter 3)

The Business Activity Model should drive Requirements Definition in the area of functional requirements.

Functional requirements are defined explicitly in terms of information support for business activities. Non-functional requirements may be derived from the measures of performance specified in the Business Activity Model.

2.4.2 Data Flow Modelling (covered in the Function Modelling volume)

Business Activity Modelling influences the role of the Current Physical Data Flow Model:

- the Current Physical Data Flow Model (DFM) provides one route for discovering the business activities - "this is what we do now - what business activities are we supporting?";

- Business Activity Modelling provides a more systematic approach to investigating the possibilities of reuse of parts of existing systems. It investigates the business requirements and can be used to evaluate the Current Physical Data Flow Model, asking the question "is what we are doing now adequate to support the business need?". Even where existing code cannot be re-used, specifications may be re-usable.

The use of Current Physical Data Flow Models allows the analyst to understand the detail of what is currently happening in the area under investigation and provides a means of checking with the user what data is being used and what processes are being performed. However, it often causes problems when the analyst is required to take an objective view of the underlying data and processes during logicalisation as this requires a complete switch in thinking. The development of a Business Activity Model approaches the system from an entirely different viewpoint and allows the analyst to model the essential activities of the system without becoming too involved in the detail of what is actually going on. These two different views are both very useful and can be used to complement one another in the investigation of the system.

2.4.3 *Logical Data Modelling (covered in the* Data Modelling *volume)*

The requirements for information support to the Business Activity Model will provide a direct set of requirements for the Logical Data Model. Initially, the Business Activity Model will help to identify the data that should be covered in the Current Environment Logical Data Model and later will help to identify data that is needed in the Required System Logical Data Model.

The Business Activity Model for a project will have a defined scope within a broader business picture. There may be a Corporate Data Model to support this broader view of the business, with which the project Logical Data Model must be reconciled.

2.4.4 *Entity Behaviour Modelling (covered in the* Behaviour and Process Modelling *volume)*

When the information support that is required to support the Business Activity Model has been investigated, it should be possible to identify the way in which the Business Events cause the Logical Data Model to be updated and identify which business activities can provide the inputs.

2.4.5 *Work Practice Modelling (covered in the* User Centred Design *volume)*

The Work Practice Model is a mapping of the Business Activity Model on to an organisation to specify:

- who (which user roles) carry out each business activity;
- where the activities are carried out.

3   REQUIREMENTS DEFINITION

Requirements Definition establishes functional and non-functional requirements for the proposed system. Its objectives are to:

- identify requirements for the proposed system which meet the needs of users, and of the business as a whole;

- describe requirements in quantifiable terms;

- provide a basis for decisions about the new system;

- ensure analysis is focused on requirements for the future system;

- provide a basis for acceptance criteria.

Its end-product is the Requirements Catalogue, developed in Investigation and used by all other parts of the System Development Template, as illustrated in Figure 3-1.

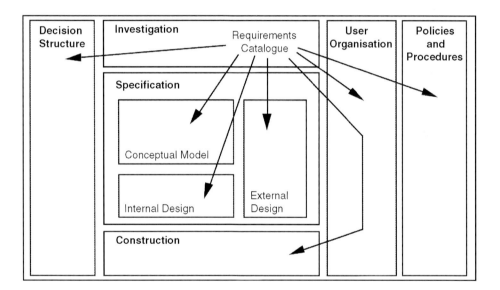

Figure 3-1 The Requirements Catalogue in the System Development Template

A fundamental principle is that the IT system is developed for support of user jobs – business activities, grouped into tasks, carried out by user roles which are assigned to people in the organisation. In general, the IT requirement is derived from the job, not vice versa.

Requirements Definition is iterative, addressing requirements in increasing detail as the project progresses. Deciding how much detail is required at any given point is a matter of judgement rather than formal technique.

Requirements should always be described in terms which:

- can be measured;

- are detailed enough to reduce ambiguity and to base decisions on;

- minimise duplication across the various specification products;

- can be tested against and thus usable as acceptance criteria.

3.1 Concepts of Requirements Definition

There are two types of requirement that need to be defined and documented. These are:

- Functional Requirements;

- Non-Functional Requirements.

3.1.1 Functional Requirements

Functional Requirements are those for facilities and features needed to satisfy the information needs of the user. Basically they cover "what " the system should do.

Types of functional requirements are:

- **Updates**; in EU-Rent this could be "accept car rental details", "log return of car" or "acknowledge sale of car";

- **Enquiries**; in EU-Rent this could be "show all bookings for tomorrow" or "show details of car groups";

- **Reports**; in EU-Rent this could be "print out all bookings taken in the last week" or "print out a list of all cars scheduled for service";

- **Interactions with other systems**; in EU-Rent this could be "Transfer all credit card transactions to the central VISA system".

Functional Requirements are the basic requirements for the new system. Generally speaking it is easy to get the user to provide details of Functional Requirements.

3.1.2 Non-Functional Requirements

Non-Functional Requirements describe how well the new system should work. These include:

- service level requirements;

- access restrictions;

- security;

- monitoring;
- audit and control;
- conversion from current system;
- interfaces with other systems;
- archiving;
- usability.

Service level requirements

Facilities of the system are provided to the user as 'services'. Service level requirements are measures of the quality of service required and are crucial to capacity planning and physical design.

Requirements Definition aims to identify realistic, measurable target values for each service level requirement, giving any minimum, maximum or acceptable range of values and indicating ways in which these values may fluctuate. It is to be expected that at first, users will only be able to provide 'ball-park' figures. Nevertheless these can be developed as the project progresses.

Service level requirements can act as a basis for the development of Service Level Agreements covering the ongoing provision of a service and agreed between user and IT provider.

Examples of service level requirements which should be considered include:

- service hours – time that a service is to be live including any special conditions for weekend, bank holidays, etc;
- service availability – proportion of time a service should actually be available for use, expressed as percentage of service hours;
- responsiveness – response times for on-line systems; turnaround time for batch systems;
- arrival rate – number of transactions per hour;
- throughput – total amount of work processed per unit of time, for example, number of records accessed or modified per hour;
- earliest start/latest finish of batch job;
- reliability.

Access restrictions

Access Restriction requirements should include:

- which data needs protection?

- does read or update access to a data item (for example) need to be restricted to particular User Roles?

- what level of restriction is required, for example; physical; password; encryption.

Security

Security requirements should include:

- back-up of data;

- recovery;

- fallback;

- contingency planning.

Monitoring

Monitoring requirements should include:

- what level of performance monitoring is required?

- what reports are required and how often?

- is there a requirement to monitor levels of use in the system?

Audit and control

Audit and Control requirements should include:

- are there financial audit requirements?

- what requirements are there for system audit?

- what are the requirements for performance audit?

- what facilities are required for identifying inconsistencies (e.g. pointers to non-existent records) in data organisation?

- are there requirements for controls to ensure data is handled correctly?

Conversion from current system

The analyst must identify any special requirements for conversion. For example, it may be important that no degradation of service is experienced whilst conversion is taking place.

Interfaces with other systems

If there is a need to interface with other systems, the requirements for this interface should be identified.

Archiving

Archiving requirements should include:

- how long is out-of-date data needed on the live system before it is archived?

- what data must be archived and what might be deleted?

- what might trigger the need for archive?

Usability

Much of what constitutes usability of the system is actually rooted in work practice – responsibilities, variety of work, ease of interaction with colleagues. If user jobs are well-designed, usability requirements are mainly concerned with:

- scope of functions;

- ergonomics;

- help;

- performance.

3.2 Product of Requirements Definition – The Requirements Catalogue

The Requirements Catalogue is the central repository for information about requirements and provides a flexible tool for recording and tracking requirements. It is created at the start of Requirements Analysis, or may be provided from an earlier Feasibility Study. Initially requirements might be recorded only in general terms in the Requirements Catalogue. As the project progresses the Requirements Catalogue is extended and refined as new requirements are identified and more detail is added.

As the project progresses, the Requirements Catalogue may grow too large to handle as a single product. It may have to be structured into smaller units based, for example, on business areas or subsystems.

The Requirements Catalogue is supported by the Business Activity Model and should always be focused on the future, although requirements may be derived from problems in current systems.

Ideally, the Requirements Catalogue should be a view of the repository used by the project's CASE tool(s), so that its requirements can then be traced through to solutions via automatic links to specification and design products. If this level of automated support is not available, the Requirements Catalogue is often maintained on a word processor, and cross references between its entries and CASE repository items maintained manually.

Both functional and non-functional requirements are recorded in the Requirements Catalogue. The information that should be recorded for each requirement includes the following:

Requirement ID   a unique identifier

Requirement name   descriptive name for the requirement

Business activity	enter the name of the business activity supported by this requirement
Source	enter the source(s) of the requirement. This may be a person, document, etc.
Priority	enter a priority for the requirement, defined by the user, and described for example as high/low, or mandatory/desirable/optional
Owner	enter the user or user organisation with ownership and responsibility for negotiation about the requirement
Functional requirement	enter a description of a facility or feature that is required
Non-functional requirement	enter a description of non-functional requirements and where possible identify target value, acceptable range (including any maximum or minimum values), and any qualifying comments
Benefits	briefly describe the benefits expected from meeting the requirement
Comments/suggested solutions	note any possible solutions to the requirement and general comments (possibly cross-referred to critical success factors)
Related documents	enter a reference to any related documents
Related requirements	if different requirements influence each other or conflict they should be cross referenced so any variation in one can be assessed with reference to the impact on the other
Resolution	make a note of how a requirement will be resolved. If a decision is made not to pursue a requirement, for example, the reasons should be recorded.

An example of a Requirements Catalogue Entry taken from the EU-Rent System is shown in Figure 3-2.

Requirement ID	0123
Requirement Name	Free rentals from benefit system
Business Activity	Free Rental
Source	Customer benefits system
Priority	Mandatory, but not so urgent as support for primary operations - rentals and maintenance.
Owner	Benefits programme administration manager
Functional requirement	Accept a reservation for a rental that will be paid for by points accumulated by a customer in the benefits system. Only basic rental charge will be covered by the benefits system. Other charges will be charged to the customer's credit card.
Non-functional Requirements	Reservations must be submitted at least two weeks before the rental start date. Telephone reservations must be confirmed immediately; this requires a response time of 10 seconds or less.
Benefits	This requirement is an essential element of the customer benefits system to which EU-Rent management has committed.
Comments/suggested solutions	Reservations could be handled by the pick-up branch, a central section, or both. Functionally, they could be combined with advance reservations for paid rentals. Postal applications are allowed so they could be processed off-line.
Related documents	Business Activity Process 7 covers benefits scheme Business Activity Process 2 covers account membership of
Related requirements	0122 Admission to benefits scheme - determines eligibility 0067 Rental Return - credits/debits points to the benefit scheme
Resolution	Handled by the entity *Free Rental*, the event *Reservation* and the function *Accept Rental Request*.

Figure 3-2 Example Requirements Catalogue Entry

3.3   The Requirements Definition Technique

The activities undertaken in Requirements Definition are illustrated in Figure 3-3 and described in the following paragraphs.

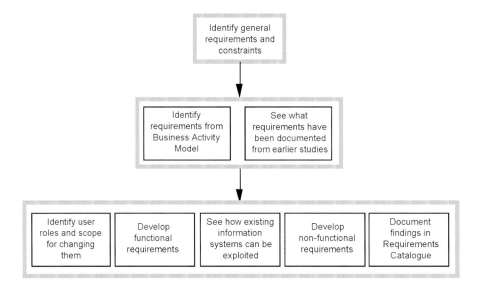

Figure 3-3 Requirements Definition activities

3.3.1 Identify general requirements and constraints

General requirements are global constraints and requirements for the project. They may be project-specific interpretations of general standards for the organisation, such as requirements to conform with corporate standards for dealing with customers and the general public.

They might include the need for the project to fit strategic plans for IS development or overall objectives for the business area under investigation.

3.3.2 Identify requirements from Business Activity Model

The Business Activity Model (see Chapter 2) should be used to identify requirements for support in most of the following areas:

- information support for operational activities;
- obligations on business activities to provide IS updates;
- communication between business activities;
- communication with the outside world;
- potential for automation of some business activities;
- collection and presentation of performance data;
- decision support for control action.

3.3.3 See what requirements have been documented from earlier studies

There may be a partially developed Requirements Catalogue developed in earlier work; for example, in a Feasibility Study or strategy report.

3.3.4 Identify user roles and the scope for changing them

The scope for changing user roles is an important factor in Requirements Definition, Business System Options and Work Practice Modelling. Some projects have to provide IT services for user roles that cannot be changed significantly (for example, because user roles are already determined by participation in other systems); the only changes permitted are in the operational detail of how business activity is done and how IT services are used. Requirements will be mainly focused on IT support.

Some projects have authority to redefine user roles to improve work practice (e.g., remove duplicated activity, reduce the number of participants in a business transaction, simplify communication between participants), or maximise exploitation of IT. Requirements will cover both IT support and work practice. There may be a wide range of options available with different impacts on the organisation and different costs and benefits. It is important in Requirements Definition to confine the scope to solutions that would be practicable in the organisation. It may be necessary to conduct a Feasibility Study to narrow the range of options before carrying out detailed requirements definition.

3.3.5 Develop functional requirements

IT services that functional requirements have to deliver are determined by the Business Activity.

Business activities need information to support them, which could come from three sources:

- the information system, part of which is the designed IT;
- the external environment;
- directly from other business activities.

The Requirements Catalogue documents requirements that will be satisfied by the designed IT system, including access to other automated systems.

As well as support of operational activities, functional requirements for information support must also cover:

- monitoring of performance of business activities against expectations; what information is to be collected and whether it is to be reported immediately or retained in the IT system;
- support for activities for resolution of conflict and control action, which usually involve human judgement and generally cannot be automated. They usually need

enquiries, browsing, 'data mining', perhaps decision support, extracts imported by local tools (spreadsheets, etc.) for 'what if' modelling.

Triggering of output from the IT system may be required to be initiated by the user, as on-line enquiries or on-request reports. Alternatively, output may be triggered by the system, as automatic prompts when specified conditions occur or as scheduled reports.

Stored data has to be maintained in order to deliver the required information. Some business activities have responsibilities to provide input to the database. Functional requirements include updating of the database and the types of input needed to do so.

3.3.6 See how existing IT systems can be exploited

There may be opportunities (or requirements) to use components of existing IT systems (sometimes known as Legacy Systems), by :

- interfacing with them;

- inheriting and migrating their data;

- replacing them, but reusing parts of them, such as formats and program modules.

Use (or potential use) of existing systems should be documented in 'Comments/suggested solutions' entries in the Requirements Catalogue.

Some non-functional requirements may address problems in current systems. It has to be established whether they are problems of what the system is doing or how it is doing it.

3.3.7 Develop non-functional requirements

Non-functional requirements describe how, how well, or to what level of quality a facility or group of facilities should be provided. Addressing non-functional requirements, such as service level requirements for performance and availability, is central to the success of the system.

Non-functional requirements may address the system as a whole or relate to particular facilities. The scope of non-functional requirements is indicated by their association with particular functional requirements. For example, a response time might be associated with an enquiry. If appropriate the analyst should indicate that a non-functional requirement is 'system-wide' or relates to a group of facilities.

The scope of non-functional requirements should be continuously reviewed. For example, users may initially indicate a requirement for a high level of availability over the entire system. Further analysis may reveal this to be only necessary for part of the system.

3.3.8 Document findings in the Requirements Catalogue

The Requirements Catalogue provides a flexible means of recording and tracking requirements but, since entries are expressed in natural language, it is not sufficient in itself for the precise specification of the required system. Later in the project, a number of more rigorous techniques including Function Definition, Logical Data Modelling and Entity Behaviour Modelling will be used to model the required system in detail, drawing on entries in the Requirements Catalogue. The resulting package of products provides a complete specification of requirements.

Later in the project the Requirements Catalogue will be reviewed to see which entries are addressed using other techniques and products. For example, a requirement to update a database will be documented as a Function Definition. Processing requirements will be further developed using Entity Behaviour Modelling. Entries in the Requirements Catalogue should be clearly cross referenced to other products to retain traceability for the purpose of validation. If the Requirements Catalogue cannot be maintained in the repository for the project's CASE tool, traceability will require manually maintained cross referencing.

3.3.9 Quantifying requirements

It is important to ensure that, wherever possible, requirements are defined in terms that are quantifiable and measurable. For example, service level requirements should be given a target and/or an acceptable range of values, which may be based on current performance. This helps to reduce ambiguity and provides a basis for testing whether the implemented system meets requirements as specified.

Quantifying requirements serves two purposes - to agree what is required from the system, and to prove that the required system was delivered. Quantified requirements will be used as criteria for acceptance and conformance tests in quality assurance and in post-implementation reviews.

Even relatively subjective requirements can be measured, although the means may not be immediately obvious. In EU-Rent, for example, there is a requirement to maintain customer satisfaction. While this does not appear to lend itself to measurement, it is possible to devise criteria – number of complaints per month for example – which will later enable users to assess whether the requirement is being met by the system.

3.4 Relationship with other analysis and design techniques

The Requirements Catalogue is the central repository of information about requirements and can feed into or be updated by any technique or product. Requirements definition has a particular role in relation to the following techniques.

3.4.1 Business Activity Modelling (covered in Chapter 2)

The Business Activity Model is a major source of requirements. The information needed to support each business activity is identified; much of this information is required from the new IT system. The Business Activity Model should identify requirements for support in most of the following areas:

- information support for operational activities;

- obligations on business activities to provide IS updates;

- communication between business activities;

- communication with the outside world;

- potential for automation of some business activities;

- collection and presentation of performance data;

- decision support for control action.

Functional requirements are specified to support business activities. The Business Activity Model's needs for information support are the source of most functional requirements.

3.4.2 Work Practice Modelling (covered in the User Centred Design volume)

The scope for changing user roles is a important factor in Requirements Definition and Work Practice Modelling. Where projects have authority to redefine user roles to improve work practice, requirements will cover both IT support and work practice.

3.4.3 Data Flow Modelling (covered in the Function Modelling volume)

Modelling the current environment using Data Flow Diagrams (DFDs) can help identify requirements arising from current problems. The Required System Data Flow Model describes required functionality and, along with the Requirements Catalogue, is input to Function Definition.

3.4.4 Function Definition (covered in the Function Modelling and User Centred Design volumes)

The Requirements Catalogue will identify requirements for enquiries and updates. Function Definition takes these requirements and defines them more rigorously by beginning to define the processing required.

On-line functions are covered as part of *User Centred Design*, whilst off-line (batch) functions are covered as part of *Function Modelling*.

3.4.5 Logical Data Modelling (covered in the Data Modelling volume)

During Requirements Definition, new requirements may be identified which need additional data items, entities and relationships. Such requirements should be recorded in the Requirements Catalogue and subsequently modelled using the Logical Data Modelling technique. The Required System Logical Data Model ensures the system will be able to support the data requirements of users.

3.4.6 Business System Options(covered in the SSADM Foundation volume)

The Requirements Catalogue feeds into the process of defining and selecting Business System Options, indicating functional requirements, priorities and expected benefits for the new system (full details of non-functional requirements are not essential although broad constraints, security requirements, etc., should be available).

3.4.7 Technical System Options

As part of the Requirements Specification, the Requirements Catalogue feeds into the process of defining Technical System Options. System-wide features, constraints and other requirements for the technical environment are considered in the definition of Technical System Options.

4   META-MODEL FOR THE BUSINESS CONTEXT

The purpose of the meta-model is to explain the concepts of Business Activity Modelling and Requirements Definition. This model attempts to identify the key concepts of these areas and shows the interrelationships between the concepts.

The meta-model diagram is shown in Figure 4-1. Some points to note about the model are as follows:

- the concept of 'Requirement' is not linked to any of the other concepts on the model. This is because in order to model all possible links between 'Requirement' and its related concepts it would require links to be made to almost every other concept on the model which would be of limited value;

- 'Business Rule' is assumed to be a compound concept which may require a number of individual rules to be invoked in order to be a complete statement. For example, in EU-Rent, individual rules could be that a valid driving licence is required and that the potential driver needs to be over 25 for the business rule which governs who will be permitted to rent a car;

- each 'Trigger to Business Activities' can invoke one or more business activities. Each trigger is one of the following:

  - a 'Business Event';

  - a stimulus from another business activity indicated by the 'Dependency' concept.

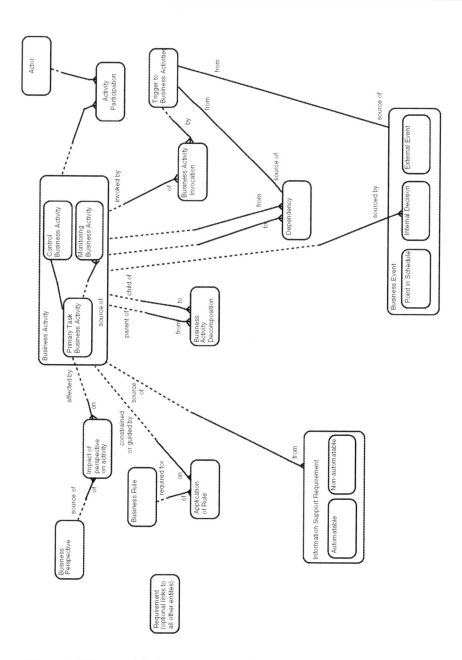

Figure 4-1 Meta-model of concepts covered by the Business Context

Entity	Description
Business Activity	A transformation in the business system which acts on inputs to produce outputs. Business activities can be dependent on other business activities, they can be triggered by business events and are performed by actors in the business system. Business activities can be broken down hierarchically into component business activities.
Business Activity Decomposition	Relationship between two business activities whereby one is part of the decomposition of the other.
Business Event	A happening in the business context to which the business system has to react. It will always be associated with a trigger which activates one or more business activities. It may be the source of events to which the automated system needs to respond.
Business Perspective	A perspective, perception, outlook or belief about what the business is, should be or should be based on. This is not necessarily held by a single person and will not be the only perspective of a particular person.
Business Rule	For many business activities there are explicit rules for how activities are done. Rules are of two types – constraints and operational guidance.
Control Business Activity	A type of business activity which analyses a primary task business activity's performance and reacts where objectives are not met to change the activity or the resources or rules used by the activity.
Dependency	Relationship between two business activities such that one activity cannot be executed successfully without the supply of a controlling message, information or resource from the other.
Information Support Requirement	The Business Activity Model represents a system of business activities which will be supported by an information system. The information system covers all the stored information that is needed by business activities and can contain non-automated information sources as well as IT support. A requirement for information support identifies the need for specific information required to execute a particular business activity. Automatable requirements are likely to identify requirements for enquiries from the new system.
Monitoring Business Activity	A type of business activity that exists solely in order to collect information from primary task business activities in order to compare actual figures with targets.
Primary Task Business Activity	A type of business activity which contributes to the overall objective of the system. For example, in the EU-Rent system the Primary Task activities will be concerned with renting and charging for rental of cars.

Entity	Description
Requirement	Describes a required feature of the proposed system. Requirements may be functional (describing what the system should do) and/or non-functional (describing how a facility should be provided, or how well, or to what level of quality). Documented as part of Requirements Definition in the Requirements Catalogue.
Trigger to Business Activities	An activator of one or more business activities. A trigger will either be an event or a dependency from another business activity.

5   PRODUCT DESCRIPTIONS FOR THE BUSINESS CONTEXT

5.1   Business Activity Model

5.1.1 Purpose

To explicitly model what goes on in the business, with a view to identifying what is to be supported by the information system.

To enable the analyst to develop requirements, directly from the needs of business activities.

To ensure that the design of the IT system will be user-centred; the services that the IT system will provide will be designed to support the business activities, rather than the IT system-centred view that a set of enquiries and updates has to be provided, to be used as needed by authorised users.

5.1.2 Composition

There is not a precise definition of what the Business Activity Model should look like. However, it should include:

- **Business** Perspectives; statement(s) of belief of what the business is trying to achieve;

- **Logical Activity Model;** what activities are carried out in the business and the dependencies between them; a distinction should be made between business and IS activities;

- **Business Events** and the business activities triggered when they occur;

- **Business Rules** – constraints and operational guidance – that determine how business activities are done.

In addition, it is important to document the beliefs, assumptions and perspectives that are used to identify critical success factors.

5.1.3 Position in System Development Template

Investigation.

5.1.4 Quality Criteria:

1   Are business activities defined independent of the user organisation?

2   Are business activities that are to be automated specified unambiguously and in sufficient detail to be used in later parts of the project?

3   Are all the business events which trigger business activities clearly identified?

4   Are the business rules consistent with organisational policies and relevant legislation?

5.1.5 External Dependencies

None

5.2   Requirements Catalogue

5.2.1 Purpose

To package details of all requirements, both functional and non-functional, identified at a particular time during the project.

Each entry in the Requirements Catalogue provides the description of a requirement for the proposed new system. Requirements are recorded in the Requirements Catalogue and updated throughout analysis and design activities to ensure a full, quantified expression of requirements. It may be necessary to baseline some of the requirements so that the system can be designed, implemented and tested against a solid set of requirements.

The Requirements Catalogue is the essential repository of requirements, from initial inception through to acceptance testing, and should be maintained throughout the entire system development.

5.2.2 Composition

Each Requirements Catalogue entry consists of:

- Requirement identification details
  - Source of requirement
  - Priority of requirement
  - Owner of requirement
  - Requirement identifier;
- Functional Requirement description;
- Non-functional requirement(s) details – repeating group consisting of
  - Description
  - Target value
  - Acceptable range
  - Comments;
- Benefits;
- Comments/suggested solution;
- Related documents;
- Related requirements;
- Resolution.

5.2.3 Position in System Development Template

Principally Investigation – used throughout.

5.2.4 Quality Criteria:

For each requirement:

1. Is the description of each functional requirement as complete as possible?

2. Are non-functional requirements as fully documented as possible?

3. Have source, owner, priority and benefit been identified?

For the complete set of requirements:

4. Does the Requirements Catalogue describe all identified requirements of the new system?

5. Are requirements consistent with the project objectives ?

6. Have all necessary previous requirements been carried forward?

5.2.5 External Dependencies

Requirements are discussed with relevant users.

Relevant users/owners are represented on the Review Team.

ANNEXE A – DESCRIPTION OF SYSTEM DEVELOPMENT TEMPLATE

The System Development Template (SDT) provides a common structure for the overall system development process. This template is used extensively in the definition of SSADM.

The System Development Template divides the development process into a number of distinct areas of concern, as shown in the diagram below.

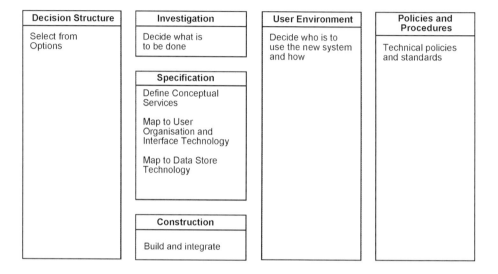

Figure A-1 System Development Template general view

The 3-schema specification architecture (which covers the Specification area) concentrates on those products that will ultimately lead, sometimes via other products, into elements of software. The SDT takes a broader view and divides the system development process into activity areas onto which all the development products may be mapped.

ANNEXE B – DESCRIPTION OF EU-RENT CASE STUDY

EU-Rent is a car rental company owned by EU-Corporation. It is one of three businesses – the other two being hotels and an airline – that each have their own business and IT systems, but share their customer base. Many of the car rental customers also fly with EU-Fly and stay at EU-Stay hotels.

EU-Rent business

EU-Rent has 1000 branches in towns all over Europe. At each branch cars, classified by car group, are available for rental. Each branch has a manager and booking clerks who handle rentals.

Rentals

Most rentals are by advance reservation; the rental period and the car group are specified at the time of reservation. EU-Rent will also accept immediate ('walk-in') rentals, if cars are available.

At the end of each day cars are assigned to reservations for the following day. If more cars have been requested than are available in a group at a branch, the branch manager may ask other branches if they have cars they can transfer to him/her.

Returns

Cars rented from one branch of EU-Rent may be returned to any other branch. The renting branch must ensure that the car has been returned to some branch at the end of the rental period. If a car is returned to a branch other than the one that rented it, ownership of the car is assigned to the new branch.

Servicing

EU-Rent also has service depots, each serving several branches. Cars may be booked for maintenance at any time provided that the service depot has capacity on the day in question.

For simplicity, only one booking per car per day is allowed. A rental or service may cover several days.

Customers

A customer can have several reservations but only one car rented at a time. EU-Rent keeps records of customers, their rentals and bad experiences such as late return, problems with payment and damage to cars. This information is used to decide whether to approve a rental.

Current IT system

Each branch and service depot has a local IT system based on PCs and a file server. The equipment is obsolete and limited in capacity (especially RAM). Hardware failures – screens, disk drives and power supplies – are increasingly frequent. There is currently no use of the Internet either for customer to business communication or for business to business communication.

Application maintainability

The application programs have been maintained over several years. Small RAM in the PCs has necessitated intricate, complex programs which makes amendments progressively more difficult and expensive.

Informal communication

Each location operates almost independently of others. Communication between locations is mainly by phone and fax and co-ordination is very variable. Sometimes, when a car is dropped off at a branch different from the pick-up branch, the drop-off branch will not inform the pick-up branch.

Branch managers tend to co-operate in small groups and not to look for 'spare' cars outside those groups. EU-Rent management feels that some capacity is wasted, but does not have reliable estimates of how much.

Scheduling of service bookings in branch and service depot files is co-ordinated by faxes between branch and depot. Sometimes service bookings are not recorded in the branch files, and cars booked for servicing are rented. Service depots sometimes do not get to know that a car has been transferred to a branch served by other depots until another depot requests the car's service history.

Customer blacklist

A copy of the customer blacklist is held at every branch. It should be updated every week from head office, but the logistics of updating the list with input from 1000 sources and sending out 1000 disks every week are beyond head office's capability. Updates are in fact sent out about every four weeks.

E-Commerce

There is no current use of e-commerce with customers having to phone or fax the individual offices to book cars for rental. This is causing problems in that some competitors have introduced facilities that enable customers to book and monitor their bookings over the Internet and it is thought that this is resulting in a loss of custom.

IT system replacement

EU-Rent management has decided that a new IT system is needed. It is expected whilst the basic operational activity is not expected to change significantly – locations and volume of rentals – it is expected that a number of 'online' systems (e.g. ordering of cars) will be implemented not necessarily as part of the initial role out but shortly thereafter. The new system is justified on three grounds:

- the current system cannot be kept going much longer;

- the perceived need to introduce some online system that can be accessed directly by customers over the Internet;

- better management of numbers of cars at branches and better co-ordination between branches is expected to increase utilisation of cars slightly – the same volume of business should be supportable with fewer cars. Each car ties up about 8,000 Euros in capital and loses about 3,000 Euros in depreciation, so significant savings are possible from small reductions in numbers of cars needed.

Corporate data

After the current IT system has been replaced, EU-Rent management wants to explore possibilities for sharing customer data across the car rental, hotel and airline systems. Even if customers are not stored in a single shared database, it makes sense for all three business areas to have consistent customer information on current address, telephone number, credit rating, etc.

It will be useful to know in each system when there are problems with a customer in other systems. And it may be possible to run promotions in one system, based on what EU-Corporation knows from the other systems about customers.

Future requirements

A customer loyalty incentive scheme is also under consideration. The requirement is not yet precisely defined but the scheme will be comparable with those offered by EU-Rent's competitors.

Members of the scheme will accumulate credit points with each car rental. They will exchange points for 'free' rentals. Only the base rental price will be payable by points; extra charges such as insurance and fuel will be paid for by cash or credit card. When this is introduced it is expected that customers will wish to be able to check (either by the use of a call-centre or directly over the Internet) the current state of their credit points.

Rationale for EU-Rent

The business of EU-Rent is car rentals, but this is largely irrelevant; it merely provides an easily understood context for examples. The business issues and user requirements in EU-Rent could be easily mapped to other systems. They include:

- a requirement to deliver a range of services (rental of cars of different quality and price) at many locations (rental branches), with different volumes of business and patterns of demand;

- customers who may use more than one location, but whose business with the whole organisation should be tracked;

- strong general policies set centrally (car models that may be used, rental tariffs, procedures for dealing with customers), but significant flexibility and authority for local managers (number of cars owned by branch, authority to over-ride published tariff to beat competitors' prices);

- a requirement for customers to be able to directly access aspects of the system;

- performance targets for local managers;

- a requirement for capacity planning and resource replenishment (disposal and purchase of cars, moving of cars between branches); possibilities for this to be managed locally, regionally or centrally;

- locally-managed sharing or swapping of resources or customers between branches to meet short-term unforeseen demand;

- an internal support structure (the maintenance depots) needed to maintain the resources and ensure that the product delivered to customers is of adequate quality;

- a customer base that is shared with other, separate systems (EU-Stay hotels and EU-Fly airline), and possibilities of communicating or co-ordinating with these systems.

Many of these characteristics are common to other types of business; for example, health care, vocational training, social security, policing, retail chain stores, branch banking.

ANNEXE C – GLOSSARY OF TERMS

access restriction non-functional requirement

A type of non-functional requirement in the Requirements Catalogue which covers the following:

- which data needs protection?

- does read or update access to a data item (for example) need to be restricted to particular User Roles?

- what level of restriction is required, for example, physical; password; encryption.

actor

Whoever, or whatever, is responsible for performing a business activity. An actor can be human or computer.

ad-hoc enquiry

An enquiry which is not pre-defined but is created by the user as and when it is needed.

business activity

A transformation in the business system which acts on inputs to produce outputs. Business activities can be dependent on other business activities, they can be triggered by business events and are performed by actors in the business system. Business activities are the major components of a Business Activity Model. Where a business activity requires information support or is a candidate for automation, this will give rise to requirements in the Requirements Catalogue.

Business Activity Model

A Business Activity Model describes business activities, business events and business rules.

There is not a precise definition of what the Business Activity Model should look like. However, it should include:

- **Business Perspectives**; statement(s) of belief of what the business is trying to achieve;

- **Logical Activity Model;** what activities are carried out in the business and the dependencies between them; a distinction should be made between business and IS activities;

- **Business Events** and the business activities triggered when they occur;

- **Business Rules** – constraints and operational guidance – that determine how business activities are done.

Whatever approach has been used, the model may be validated by comparing it against a formal model of a Human Activity System as defined by Checkland.

Business Activity Modelling

There are a wide range of methods and techniques available to analysts for modelling business activities. Whatever technique is chosen, it should aim to produce a Business Activity Model as defined above.

business event

A business event is a trigger which activates one or more business activities.

Business events are of three types:

- external inputs – inputs from outside the system boundary;

- decisions made in business activities within the system;

- scheduled points in time.

A business event may trigger more than one activity. A business activity may be triggered by more than one business event.

business perspective

Statement(s) of belief of what the business is trying to achieve. A single perspective can be shared by many different people and each person can subscribe to more than one perspective.

business rules

For many business activities there are explicit rules for how activities are done. Wherever rules are available, they should be referenced from the business activities. Rules are of two types – constraints and operational guidance.

business thread

A business thread can be recognised as the path through a set of business activities which are the outcome of an initiating business event. A thread does not need to be continuous in its progression, but may need further business events to trigger later business activities.

Capacity Planning

A technique used to predict the (hardware/software) configuration required to satisfy the constraints and requirements of the proposed system.

It is also used to assist in the development of service level agreements.

Checkland's formal system model

A formal model of a Human Activity System as defined by Checkland, in which the following mandatory elements are defined:

- Objectives and purpose;

- Connectivity;

- Measures of performance;

- Monitoring and control mechanisms;

- Decision-taking procedures;

- Boundary;

- Resources;

- Systems hierarchy.

For more details see Systems Thinking, Systems Practice by Peter Checkland (published by Wiley, ISBN: 0 471 27911 0)

constraint non-functional requirement

A type of non-functional requirement in the Requirements Catalogue which covers the following:

- Conversion from current system;

- Interfaces with other systems;

- Human – computer interface requirements;

- Archiving.

Feasibility Report

This is the product which documents the possible approaches to the system development and assesses the impact of each so that the most appropriate way ahead can be fully investigated.

Human Activity System

A Human Activity System is the system modelled by Business Activity Modelling. A Human Activity System is a coherent set of activities and the logical dependencies between them; it describes what has to be done in a business, as distinct from who does it and how it is done. It can be mapped on to an organisation structure to define a business system. In the mapping to an organisation, some of the activities in the Human Activity System may be automated. A Human Activity System needs information support, which is specified separately from the Human Activity System. Usually, only part of the information support will be provided by an IT system.

information support

The requirements for information specified by business activities. Information support can cover all types of information needed to execute business activities, including unstructured data and structured data. Requirements for information support are used as the basis for identifying enquiries and will help to specify what data should be provided by the Logical Data Model.

Logical Data Model

Provides an accurate model of the information requirements of all or part of an organisation. This serves as a basis for file and database design, but is independent of any specific implementation technique or product.

The Logical Data Model consists of a Logical Data Structure, Entity Descriptions and Relationship Descriptions. Associated descriptions of attribute/data items and domains are maintained in the Data Catalogue.

monitoring non-functional requirement

A type of non-functional requirement which covers the following:

- what level of performance monitoring is required?
- what reports are required and how often?
- is there a requirement to monitor levels of use in the system?

non-functional requirement

A requirement which describes how, how well or to what level of quality a facility of the system should be provided. Examples include service level requirements, access restrictions, security, monitoring, audit and control, usability and constraints.

Primary Task Model

The Primary Task Model of a Human Activity System defines what the system does in order to be the one defined in the Root Definition. The Primary Task Model is a coherent set of connected activities.

A Primary Task Model is derived formally from its Root Definition, and only from its Root Definition. It should not include any real-world activities that are not represented in the Root Definition.

project

A project is regarded as having the following characteristics:

- a defined and unique set of technical products to meet the business needs;
- a corresponding set of activities to construct those products;
- a certain amount of resources;
- a finite and defined lifespan;
- an organisational structure with defined responsibilities.

quality criteria

Characteristics of a product which determine whether it meets requirements, and thus define what 'quality' means in the context of that product. These are defined in the Product Descriptions and agreed with the project board before development of the product commences.

Resource Flow Diagram

Documents how resources move within an organisation. This diagram will be produced if the current system is predominantly concerned with movement of physical objects, e.g., goods.

Root Definition

A concept used in Business Activity Modelling, particularly where the Soft Systems Methodology is used. The Root Definition is a statement of what the Human Activity System is taken to be. It incorporates a recognition that it is impossible to model all of reality and defines the Human Activity System from one of a number of different business perspectives. A Root Definition is developed for each perspective.

service level requirement

A non-functional requirement which states the required quality of service the user expects from a functional aspect of the system.

Soft Systems Methodology

The Soft Systems Methodology (SSM) is directed at modelling of Human Activity Systems.

A 'hard' system requirement is a situation in which what is needed is known and the system specification has to address how to meet the requirement. A 'soft' system requirement is a situation in which what is needed has to be defined before addressing how it can be provided.

The Soft Systems Methodology (SSM) addresses soft systems requirements. SSM is directed at business activity, and specifies IS requirements in terms of information support for business activity.

System Development Template

The System Development Template provides a common structure for the overall system development process.

It divides the process into a number of distinct areas of concern:

- Investigation;
- Specification;
- Construction;
- Decision Structure;
- User Organisation;
- Policies and Procedures.

The Specification area contains the Three-schema Specification Architecture which is made up of the areas Conceptual Model, Internal Design and External Design. The Three-schema Specification Architecture concentrates on those products that will ultimately lead, sometimes via other products, into elements of software. The System Development Template takes a broader view. It divides the system development process into activity areas onto which the development products may be mapped.

usability non-functional requirement

A type of non-functional requirement which covers the following:

- scope of functions;
- ergonomics;
- help;
- performance.

INDEX

A

B

C

monitoring business activity 44

monitoring non-functional requirements,
  definition 58

monitoring requirements 32

multiple business activities 15

N

Non-Functional Requirements 30–31, 33–35, 38
see also requirements
    definition 59
    developing 38

O

operational guidance 12–13

operational guidance, descriptions 15

organisation of this volume 6

Organisation Structure 5

P

perspectives, business 9, 13, 14, 24, 44
      conflicting 19
      definition 56

planning activities 10, 14, 25

primary task 10

primary task business activity 44

Primary Task Model 18

comparing with reality 20

definition 59

product descriptions for the business concept
  46–49

product of Requirements Definition 33–35

products of Business Activity Modelling 13–16

project, definition 59

Q

quality criteria, definition 59

R

reality, comparing with 20

reports 30

Requirement concept 42

requirements 45 *see also* Functional/Non-
  Functional Requirements
      Access Restriction 31–32
      audit and control 32
      identifying 36
      monitoring 32
      security 32
      service level 31

Requirements, Functional 30, 33–34

Requirements, Non-Functional 30–31, 33–35, 38

Requirements Catalogue 2, 29, 33–35
      composition 48
      cross referring 39
      document findings in 39
      external dependencies 49
      position in System Development Template
        49
      product description 48–49
      purpose 48
      quality criteria 49
      quantifying requirements 39
      relationship with other analysis and
        design techniques 39–41

Requirements Definition 1, 2, 27, 29–31
    activities 36
    concepts of 30–33
    product of 33–35
    technique 35–39

requirements documented from earlier studies 37

requirements for an IT project 3

resolution 34, 35

resource flow diagrams
      checklist of questions 24–25
      definition 59
      deriving business activities from 24
      deriving information categories from 24
      using 23–27

Root Definition, definition 60

Root Definitions 17, 18, 20

Rules, Business 24, 42, 44
      definition 56
      how activities are done 12–13
      set of 13, 15–16